Boxer's Bible of Counterpunching

The Killer Response to Any Attack

Mark Hatm~~~

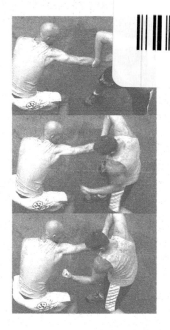

Cover and interior photos by Doug Werner

Tracks Publishing
San Diego, California

Boxer's Bible of Counterpunching
The Killer Response to Any Attack
Mark Hatmaker

Tracks Publishing
458 Dorothy Avenue
Ventura, CA 93003
805-754-0248
tracks@cox.net
trackspublishing.com

Copyright © 2012 by Mark Hatmaker and Doug Werner
10 9 8 7 6 5 4

Publisher's Cataloging-in-Publication

Boxer's bible of counterpunching : the killer response to any attack /
Mark Hatmaker ; cover and interior photos by Doug Werner. -- San
Diego, Calif. : Tracks Pub., c2012.

    p. ; cm.

    ISBN: 978-1-935937-47-0
    Meant to be used in an interlocking synergistic manner with the
author's other books in this series: Boxing mastery, and Boxer's
book of conditioning & drilling.
    Includes index.
    Summary: Boxing is more about what you do in response to
punches than punching prowess itself. This guide is an
encyclopedia of counter boxing and includes every effective
defense, response and follow-up combination to every attack.--
Publisher.

    1. Boxing. 2. Boxing--Defense. 3. Boxers (Sports)--Training.
I. Werner, Doug, 1950- II. Title.

GV1137.6 .H384 2012   2012947614
796.83--dc23   1211

Books by Mark Hatmaker

No Holds Barred Fighting:
The Ultimate Guide to Submission Wrestling

More No Holds Barred Fighting:
Killer Submissions

No Holds Barred Fighting:
Savage Strikes

No Holds Barred Fighting:
Takedowns

No Holds Barred Fighting:
The Clinch

No Holds Barred Fighting:
The Ultimate Guide to Conditioning

No Holds Barred Fighting:
The Kicking Bible

No Holds Barred Fighting:
The Book of Essential Submissions

Boxing Mastery

No Second Chance:
A Reality-Based Guide to Self-Defense

MMA Mastery:
Flow Chain Drilling and Integrated O/D Training

MMA Mastery:
Ground and Pound

MMA Mastery:
Strike Combinations

Boxer's Book of Conditioning & Drilling

Boxer's Bible of Counterpunching

Books are available through major bookstores
and booksellers on the Internet.

Dedicated to all the "Sweet Scientists" out there who have experimented and continue to experiment in the gyms and rings of the world pushing the sport and science ever further.

Acknowledgments
Phyllis Carter
Kylie Hatmaker
Mitch Thomas
Shane Tucker
Joy Werner

Contents

Warning label
The fighting arts include contact and can be dangerous. Use proper equipment and train safely. Practice with restraint and respect for your partners. Drill for fun, fitness and to improve skills. Do not fight with the intent to do harm.

> "Boxers get hit; good boxers don't get hit as much."
> — Sugar Ray Leonard

Epigraphs

Epigraphs are those cherry-picked quotations that authors use at the beginning of a book to set the stage for what is to come. I often miss the link between the epigraph and what follows, but if I do say so myself, the following two quotes sum up the mental stance I prescribe in approaching these pages. And keep in mind, these two giants of the game damn well know what they're talking about.

"Boxers get hit; good boxers don't get hit as much."
— Sugar Ray Leonard

"You can map out a fight plan or a life plan, but when the action starts, it may not go the way you planned, and you're down to your reflexes — that means your [preparation]. That's where your roadwork shows. If you cheated on that in

... there is, indeed, a wide gulf between being a puncher and being a boxer.

the dark of the morning, well, you're going to get found out now, under the bright lights."
— Joe Frazier

How to use our boxing manuals

This book and the others in this series (*Boxing Mastery* and *Boxer's Book of Conditioning & Drilling*) are meant to be used in an interlocking synergistic manner where the sum value of the manuals is greater than the individual parts. What we are striving to do with each manual is to focus on a specific aspect of the sweet science and give thoughtful consideration to the necessary ideas, tactics and strategies pertinent to the facet of focus. We are aware that this piecemeal approach may seem lacking if one consumes only one or two manuals at most, but we are confident that once several manuals have been studied, the overall picture or method will begin to reveal itself.

Since the manuals are interlocking, there is no single manual in the series that is meant to be complete in and of itself; instead, we think of each manual as an individual piece or section of a comprehensive master manual. With this volume, the Boxing Master Manual clocks in at over 600 pages. Although *Boxing Mastery* is a thorough overview on boxing, it is bolstered with side-by-side study of *Boxer's Book of Conditioning & Drilling,* which details how to train the concepts found in the first book.

The volume you hold in your hands now presumes that you have got the basics down, have honed your conditioning and are ready for the truly fun stuff — the actual science of the sweet science.

To our MMA brethren

Mixed Martial Artists you have not been forgotten! You will find much (if not all) of the material contained within of value to your game. Admittedly, we provide only encyclopedic counters for boxing attacks, but by paying attention to how we structure the drills and the tactical explanations of why we approach the drills the way we do, you should have no problem at all extrapolating to the MMA environment.

Punching v boxing

Punching versus boxing? They're the same thing, right? Or is this me asking a trick question that winds up with there being a distinction without a difference? Maybe this is one of those long-winded metaphors offered to pad pages rather than get to the meat of the topic.

I don't think so. And if I can keep your attention for a few pages, I think there's a good possibility that you'll see that there is, indeed, a wide gulf between being a puncher and being a boxer.

To highlight the differences between punching and boxing, I want you to think about the athlete who looks mighty good on the heavy bag. He's got heavy hands that give solid resounding slaps with each impact. The fighter who works a steady beat on the bag so tight that the local club could stage a rave to his beat. No bag sway, which we all know is a sign of pushing punches rather than popping punches. No sway for this guy, he's all leather impact craters. Good stuff.

You have this athlete in mind? OK, let me ask you a question: *Is this athlete a good boxer?* Huh? Now, I think you probably see where I'm

> That's where your roadwork shows. If you cheated on that in the dark of the morning, well, you're going to get found out ...
>
> — Joe Frazier

going. There's no way to tell whether or not this guy is a good boxer without actually seeing him box.

At this point you might be thinking, "OK, training on gear or training solo is not boxing training — it's punching training." You'd be close with this estimation, but there's a little more to it that that. Gear and solo training can be either boxing training or mere punch training. Let's go to another example and see if we can reveal a picture with a bit more clarity.

Let's put our fictional athlete in the ring with a sparring partner. They agree to three rounds of play. Here's what we see in each round.

Round one: Our athlete is hyper-aggressive, jabbing and throwing volley after volley that go unanswered by his sparring partner throughout. Our guy looks sharp (we must remember, looks can be deceiving).

11

> Punching is what you do to a bag or a rookie or a cooperative sparring partner. Boxing is what you do in the face of punches.

Round two: Our athlete throws a three-punch combination. His partner covers and then returns his own three-punch combination, which our athlete then covers against. And back and forth for the entire round.

Round three: Our man's sparring partner comes out with a vengeance, jabbing here, probing there and flying with some nice combinations throughout. Our man in response stays just outside the pocket, slipping, parrying, blocking, evading, staying on his bicycle and, to be honest, initiating offense only about 20 percent of the time. But ... it's what he does while he's spending 80 percent of the time defending that will define him. With practically every punch that he makes his partner miss, or with almost every impact of his partner's glove on his own defensive limb, our man fires back a response into the hole left by the offensive sparring partner's gambit.

We've got three three-minute rounds with three distinctly different flavors to evaluate now. In which rounds did we see punching and in which rounds did we see boxing?

Round one was nothing but punching. Our man simply pursued a live heavy bag and we really learned nothing about his boxing prowess.

Round two was both fighters throwing leather. Better, yes? But it was tit for tat, give and take, your turn, now mine and so on and so forth. Pretty rudimentary stuff. I mean if this qualifies as boxing, then me throwing a few spirals in the yard means I'm playing football.

So far, you can find a plethora of round one and two examples in *Toughman* competitions (a long ago boxing chum called these competitions Sloppy Slob Boxing Shows).

Round three — Ah, now here it is. Our sparring partner was in the game and good for him, but our man was r-e-s-p-o-n-s-i-v-e. He counter-punched; he fought in context with what his opponent provided. I think you can tell that round three epitomizes what I am calling the difference between punchers and boxers.

Punching is what you do when there is a) no returning fire or b) when your only plan is to impose your plan. I know some will puff up and think, "Damn, right! I want to impose my plan, what's wrong with that?"

Nothing at all, hombres. Having a plan is excellent. Chess masters have plans as well, but they don't involve making only his moves. The chess master realizes the vast portion of his plan is what he does in response to his opponent's plan. To bring it back to boxing regarding plans, a reiteration of one of our opening epigraphs and another from Iron Mike Tyson.

"You can map out a fight plan or a life plan, but when the action starts, it may not go the way you planned, and you're down to your reflexes — that means your [preparation]. That's where your roadwork shows. If you cheated on that in the dark of the morning, well, you're going to get found out now, under the bright lights."
— Joe Frazier

"Everyone has a plan until they get punched in the face." — Mike Tyson

Punching is what you do to a bag or a rookie or a cooperative sparring partner. Boxing is

Boxers don't dig new holes. Boxers concentrate their efforts on preexisting holes, or holes created by your opponent via his own actions. what you do in the face of punches.

You don't need new holes — what you're provided with are good enough That's a dodgy subheading with innuendo and double entendre written all over it. Well, what's true for the innuendo is also true for boxing. Good boxing is about analysis. That is, probing with the jab at the outset to see what sort of reactions you draw. It's about using angles and movement to see if or where your opponent moves most comfortably and where you detect a bit of awkwardness. It's about evaluating stance and movement to assess gaps in defense (both ever present gaps such as a lead hand carried too low, or potential gaps such as a straight punch that swims a bit on the return. If it swims slightly in early rounds, it will swim big once fatigue sets in).

The counter-boxer finds the holes you have already dug and fills those holes with punches.

Punchers often approach opponents as if they were trees to be chopped down, or holes (graves) to be dug. As tantalizing as these metaphors are, keep them in the world of trash talk and not as the basis of your offensive or defensive strategy.

Boxers don't chop. Boxers don't dig new holes. Boxers concentrate their efforts on preexisting holes, or holes created by your opponent via his own actions (or reactions to your actions). Let's ponder some photos to illustrate these points.

Photo #1 Here we've got a boxer in good classic guard position. Chin down, forearms parallel, rear hand to the cheek, lead hand positioned in front of the lead shoulder. Nice job, Photo #1 Boxer.

Now, what do we hit on this fighter? He's denied us his chin or a square shot to his nose. Do we waste some shots on his forehead? The ribs have good coverage. Do we burn some energy digging to the ribs all the same?

An honest assessment says if this guy remains stock still, about the only hole we have is burning one to the liver or solar plexus. Other than that, we would have to wait for him to move or use movement or probes to see what holes open up.

Photo #2 This time we've got a boxer giving us a lazy classic guard, i.e., more holes. We see the chin now, which means where hooks and uppercuts might have been wasted efforts on our Photo #1 example, here we've got a shot at landing. That chin up and the rear hand carried low also means the eyes and nose are ripe for hitting. The forearms slightly out of parallel means that the liver is a little easier to access, and short rib digging is now on the menu.

Photo #3 Look at that! Come on, really boxer in photo #3? Did someone say smorgasbord? Holes everywhere: chin, nose, temples, liver. This guy has a world of hurt coming his way.

Photo #4 In this photo we have our tight classic guard, but the jab has been launched. Compare this photo with Photo #1. No matter how tight your guard, launching an offense opens a hole somewhere. Now this fighter is still tight, he's got his chin down and buried into the shoulder of the extended punch so it's hidden. The rear hand is still carried high and tight denying us a good hook angle, but the extended hand gives us a larger hole to attack the body.

Photo #5 Here, our boxer looks like he's throwing a shovel hook to the body and a mighty loose one at that. Look at those holes — the rear hand has strayed from the cheek.

As long as your opponent moves, as long as your opponent throws a punch, you will be provided with gifts left and right.

Rather than traveling with the punch, he's allowed the lead shoulder to droop — really opening up the chin and lines for counter rear hands and hooks. The straying offensive hand opens up a big hole right over the liver.

We could continue with page after page of this photo analysis to drive home the point that offensive movement, whether thrown with good or bad technique, opens up holes in defense — it's inescapable. When you throw a punch you create a hole in your own defense no matter how tight your technique. That hole created by your offense is what the skilled counterboxer will exploit.

The counterboxer has no need of mindlessly throwing punches hoping for some solid connect. He has no need of banging on areas where there is good coverage. The counterboxer finds the holes you have already dug and fills those holes with punches.

Your job as a counterboxer — the whole point of this manual — is to educate yourself not to chop on your opponent, not to dig on your opponent, but to fill in all the holes.

It's a gift, son
Warning: Redundancy ahead!

Counterboxing is about reacting.

Counterboxing is about filling in holes.

Counterboxing is about exploiting opportunities provided by your opponent.

Counterboxing is about encouraging your opponent to provide opportunities for exploitation.

Counterboxing is a Gift System meaning you take what's provided. No need to go begging for offensive opportunities, no need for forcefully creating holes. As long as your opponent moves, as long as your opponent throws a punch, you will be provided with gifts left and right.

Your job is to hone your reactive skills so that you are fully capable of taking advantage of as many of these gifts as possible.

Armchair corner man

The following is a mighty useful little exercise that can go a long way in shifting your mindset from that of punching to boxing. That is, a mindset that sees holes to be filled. All you'll need are you and your favorite device to view fights on.

Method: Part one

Dial up a fight, any fight at all.

At random intervals in your viewing, pause the action.

Ponder both fighters and call the holes you currently see frozen on the screen.

Press play.

Rinse, wash and repeat several times per round.

Method: Part two

Once you have trained yourself to identify holes with frozen fighters, move on to calling holes live. That is, no pausing.

Ideally, I recommend calling these holes out loud (if your surroundings permit). Call each and every hole you see as they occur.

A partial transcript of this exercise might read like this.

The lead is carried low, opens up the left side of the face and temple.

His head is high when he throws the straight right, making the chin and entire right side of the head accessible.

He wings his elbows high on hooks; his ribs and liver are wide open.

When he bangs to the body, he takes his arm to the torso with no knee dip — head is wide open on the offense side.

And so on and so forth.

Method: Part 3

It's one thing to armchair it where profile viewing makes calling shots easy by mere dint of perspective (more on why in a bit). We correct that with this version of the exercise where we look for holes just as you would see them in a fight, but still no pressure on you to perform physically, just cognitively.

"Keep your hands up!" is, more often than not, Lesson One in any contact oriented combat sport, and if it isn't Lesson One or, at least Lesson Two, you might want to question that instructional tack.

Grab a boxing partner. Have your partner shadowbox a few rounds before you. He can dance, move, juke and jive to his heart's content as long as he makes the mental target of his offense and defense y-o-u.

From this center-of-attention perspective, run the same "call the holes aloud" drill.

I encourage you to try the Armchair Corner Man (all three versions) for at least a few entire fights. You will be tempted to fall into the just-view-and-enjoy habit, but here I am asking you to be

> "Knockouts aren't about power, they're about timing."
> — Sugar Ray Robinson

active — don't just see what holes either boxer fills in, look for holes that even they did not exploit. (Don't judge them harshly for their misses. I'll explain in a minute why they miss and why you'll miss more than you'll hit). By becoming adept at this cognitive exercise when you face an opponent (assuming all the other groundwork of conditioning and the basics have been laid down), you will view the situation a bit differently.

You will see holes left and right. Now, your speed, skill and/or positioning may not allow you to take advantage of all of them (or even 50 percent of them), but by merely shifting from chopping at your opponent to filling in the holes at least half of that noticed 50 percent, you should up your contact rate exponentially.

In other words, you will correct any imbalance

between the number of punches thrown and the number of punches landed.

Armchair quarterbacks be warned

I've done it, you've done it, we've all done it. You're watching the game on the big screen and you see a pass come from waaaaayy back that the receiver just doesn't see. You're thinking, "How could he possibly miss that? Is he blind? I'm not even there and I saw it from the very beginning."

Sometimes you're watching a fight and you see a fighter holding his hands up, but perhaps in a bit of an open guard and he just keeps getting peppered with punches, the jab in particular. From your viewpoint, right there in your living room, you've got no problem seeing the other fighter load up and launch. So what's up with Mr. Jab-Eater? Is this guy suffering from nerves? (Probably, a little bit and that's a wise thing, too). Is he undertrained? Outclassed? Or is he simply slow?

Well, the answer can be a bit of any of the above, but some new research from the National Academy of the Sciences demonstrates that something else may account for why we armchair quarterbacks and sofa corner men have so much "better" perceptual speed than the pros we yell at on-screen. The study's authors (Andrew E. Welchman, Judith M. Lam and Heinrich H. Bulthoff) used Bayesian motion estimation to solve this puzzle, and the root of the problem, it seems, lies in our armchair perspective.

By that I mean spectators have, by dint of being spectators, sideline seats — profile perspectives on the event in question (and from here on out we'll assume the event is a fight). Whether observing fights on TV or witnessing drills in the gym, we spend far more time in profile to the action than we spend in the path of the action. Consciously or not, as the brain observes the action, it is making estimations of the speed of the given projectile — fist, football, what have you. The profile perspective allows the observer to witness the entire arc of the projectile, a longer exposure to the motion and, thusly, calculate when a block, parry or catch can and should be timed. The brain then stores these presumptive calculations for later use when you are on the receiving end of the given projectile.

Now here's where the problem arises. The study shows that when we are in the path of

Jack Dempsey

the projectile, our spectator calculations that had benefit of the entire traveling arc are rendered inaccurate. How inaccurate? The study shows inaccurate enough to get you hit more often than not. This sentence from the study itself shows us just how dire this situation is: "Given the importance of sensing motion for obstacle avoidance, it is surprising that humans make errors, reporting that an object will miss them when it is on a collision course with their head." This study explains why we are so terrific in "seeing it all" on the sidelines, but less than stellar when we are the target.

That's the science, now let's look at just how these empirical results can impact our training. Given that we are horrible estimators of the speed of incoming objects, we might just want to discard any defensive response that requires outside-in or inside-out work and by that I mean parries of any and all sorts (here, I am referring to parrying as preemptive defense and not hands cheated into parry position — more on this distinction later). Parries presume formidable reaction speed — parries are always reactive and never proactive as they must, by their nature, "respond" to stimuli. Parries presume precognition. We presume that a strike will come in our direction, but we will never predict with certitude just when and/or what that strike might be. Parries presume the opposite of what the aforementioned scientific research demonstrates.

Sugar Ray

Don't get me wrong, I'm not quibbling with the short cuffing motions we see in professional boxing. I am referring to the sweeping movements that assume that profile perspective speed is the same as bull's-eye perspective speed. But, even with this allowance for cuffing, might there still be a safer alternative that hedges the bet for a nervous system as poorly adapted to judging incoming projectile speed as a human being's? Probably so, and it's as basic as it can get.

"Keep your hands up!" is a common admonishment from boxing coaches past, present, and more than likely, on into the distant future. "Keep your hands up!" is heard from trainers all over the world. "Keep your hands up!" is, more

often than not, Lesson One in any contact oriented combat sport, and if it isn't Lesson One
or Lesson Two, you might want to question that
instructional tack. Now, even with this prepon-
derance of good advice ("Keep your hands
up!") we still see a large percentage of fighters
discarding Lesson Numero Uno, but at least we
now have an understanding of why that might
be. Human beings are horrible estimators of
certain events. That's what keeps many of us
playing the lottery despite horrible odds, and it
seems to be what leads us to believe that we'll
"see that punch on it's way in and do something about it," evidence to the contrary be
damned.

Keeping the hands up, shoulders hunched and
tight, chin down, shortening the torso, forearms
parallel and close — this caged defensive position forms a defensive shell that eliminates the
need for parries. Keeping the hands up and
head and body in the described alignment
allows your positioning to form a defensive
cage that places less vulnerable targets (forearms, shoulders, forehead) in the path of
incoming projectiles. If we do possess formidable reactive speed, then cuffs and even parries launched from this cage position will have
to travel much less distance to be effective. But

if we build a solid defensive cage, we forgo the need for much of the cuffing, parrying gambits. We cheat our defense toward the inherent weakness of poor predictive incoming speed and keep obstructions placed between us and the strike. We only violate the integrity of the cage defense to launch our offense — an offense that is always scrupulous about returning to the cage after each strike.

By making ourselves aware of a glitch in our hardware (poor predictive incoming perspective speed) we can update our wetware (our cognitive choices) with the defensive cage and quickly get back to the job of going offensive.

The more time we spend ignoring the facts and trying to override a hardwired glitch, the more training time we waste and the more jabs we will eat and the more the armchair cornermen will wonder how we could be so blind.

Will-o'-the-wisp

Traditionally, a will-o'-the-wisp was a purported ghost encountered by travelers. It would dance, flicker and recede into the distance as witnesses attempted approach. Keep that traditional definition in mind, please.

> "Lie down so I can recognize you."
> — Willie Pep

... Pep told sportswriters that he would win the third round **without landing a punch**. And he did just that.

By the way, will-o'-the-wisps were encountered in peaty or boggy regions where decomposing vegetable matter bubbled off gases from the bottom of the slurry water. These off gases often catch receding sunlight in the twilight hours and shimmer just as one sees a wavy shimmer coming off hot asphalt in warm climes.

A few years back we lost one of the greatest boxers of all time, and I make this statement with zero hyperbole. Willie Pep was a true boxer; he had it all — footwork, speed, combinations, the whole package. We could go on all day discussing Pep's contributions to the sweet science by dint of his performance, but let's allow two oft-told tales of his work place our respect into perspective.

Pep's nickname was " Will-o'-the-wisp" because

I guess what I'm saying is, be smoke, or at the very least be Lucy and pull that football away at the last moment so you can connect when your hapless Mr. Brown is flailing at air.

of his exceptional evasion skills. This facility for artful deceptive movement was highlighted by his 1946 bout with southpaw heavy-hitter Jackie Graves. Before the fight, Pep told sportswriters that he would win the third round without landing a punch. And he did just that. Stop and ponder that — winning a round with zero offense.

Pep was in constant motion — bobbing, weaving, feinting, drawing. Name an evasive trick, and he put it on display in that round. He landed zero punches and won the round on all three judges' scorecards. He went on to knock out Graves in the eight round.

Pep's career continued to have some great battles including four fierce bouts with the tremendous Sandy Sadler. In the second bout with Sadler, the Will-o'-the-wisp was seen in speedy form again throwing 37(!) successive jabs in the first round alone. Compare that jab tally to what you most often see today.

Willie Pep and other truly brilliant counterboxers recognized that boxing — true boxing, not punching — is about timing.

Good time buddies
Let's quote another legend here:

"Knockouts aren't about power, they're about timing." — Sugar Ray Robinson

Sugar Ray knew what he was talking about. Robinson was not known as a heavy hitter and yet out of 173 wins, 108 of those were by KO. Sounds like this nonheavy hitter hit plenty hard with good timing in his bag of tricks.

We all enjoy a well-timed punch. That mighty sweet one that catches the opponent flush when his own punch is at full extension, leaving that hole wide open with his own punch biting air over your rear shoulder.

Timing is so tough to train because it requires thoughtful, cooperative drilling. You can't really train good timing on solo gear, that is until you already have drilled good timing into your brain and body via that thoughtful and cooperative drilling we just mentioned.

Building elite timing is not a solo quest because great timing is not volitional. That is, you don't get to choose the good time to throw that sweet punch we were just talking about — your opponent chooses.

Your job as a counterboxer is to be a well-trained reader of holes and potential holes who is ready to fill them when provided.

Even after you acquire good timing, it's still mighty difficult to train solo. Every punch you throw on a bag, in front of the mirror, into passive prearranged mitt patterns is self-generated and has nothing to do with timing in the true sense.

To train good timing you are simply going to have to have a good partner. It can be an active or a passive partner. An active partner is a fellow boxer who will glove up and do tit-for-tat drills with you.

Joe Louis

A passive partner is a trainer or buddy who may not necessarily want to box, but is willing to don some focus mitts and create the energy and angles required to build the enclosed timing drills.

You can build power solo, you can build speed all by your lonesome, and to some degree, you can build evasive footwork and a crafty body, but just like the tango, it takes two to perfect timing.

Video is worth 1,000,000 words

Here's another little cognitive homework assignment that doesn't call for you to even break a sweat. Turn the page and you will find a hero's gallery of legends that I consider to be mighty fine representatives of the art and science of counterboxing.

If you delve into these fighters' video archives at any point in their prime (prime being the key word, friends) you are likely to be treated to some excellent work that you should find both inspiring and perfect models of what we are striving to build with this book.

Keep in mind this is my list of folks. If your favorite fighter isn't here, by all means add him to the list and get to watching with those fingers on the pause, rewind and frame-by-frame buttons so you can see how it's done.

Jack Johnson

Ali   Jim Driscoll

Counterboxing hero's gallery
1. Sugar Ray Robinson
2. Willie Pep
3. Jack Johnson
4. Pernell Whitaker
5. Roy Jones, Jr.
6. James Toney
7. Sugar Ray Leonard
8. Winky Wright
9. Jim Driscoll
10. Richard Lopez
11. Bernard Hopkins
12. Roberto Duran (lightweight)
13. Muhammad Ali
14. Wilfredo Benitez
15. Gene Tunney
16. Jack Dempsey
17. Benny Leonard
18. Cesar Chavez

I'll rein it in at 18 since this is a game that we could play all day. Suffice to say, that's a great start. Dial up these gentlemen, sit back, watch and learn.

Don't get hit x 3

We're getting closer and closer, my friends, to the physical portion of our program. Hang with me for a bit more. There are basically only three ways to not get hit (or at least hurt) in boxing defense.

1. Don't be there.
2. Redirect
3. Put something in the way.

We will explore each of these in great detail for the remainder of the book, but in a nutshell …

1. Don't be there. Put all your evasion skills and tactics in this category — footwork, slips, weaves, bobs and the like.

2. Redirect. Any and all parries, cuffs, leverage blocks, et cetera.

3. Put something in the way. The basest form of defense, but it works — blocking. That is, absorbing a blow's impact on a portion of the anatomy not intended as the target.

Let's discuss these in detail.

The highest form of defense (and also the hardest to develop) is to be so slippery, so elusive, so evasive that your opponent feels that he might as well be punching a puff of smoke ...

Smoke

Have you heard this guy?

"I'll take two of his shots to get in my one."

Sure, you have. Don't be that guy.

Yeah, it sounds all testosteroney and cool to be that tough, but we're talking about boxing and not punching, remember? That attitude has no place in discussions of the sweet science and the artful skill of the canniest of boxers.

The elite of the elite opt to not get hit at all, if possible — it isn't. We're talking receiving zero offensive contact from the boxer in front of you. No glancing gloves off the arms or absorbing a few body shots on the folded forearms. We're talking about simply not being there when the punch arrives at where it thought it was going.

The highest form of defense (and also the hardest to develop) is to be so slippery, so elusive, so evasive that your opponent feels that he might as well be punching a puff of smoke for all of the progress he's making. Making an opponent miss is exhausting (for him) and opens a wide range of possibilities of countering as both hands are free for countering as opposed to only one, or two if you've

Good

got a speedy turnaround on your occupied defensive hand.

Making an opponent miss often causes him to pull wide, that is, open up more than intended once that target is out of the way. Good boxers know to moderate their punching for misses as they know that you will miss far more than you hit. But there is still an unavoidable openness for missing a shot when you fully expected a target impact to halt your momentum. Think of Lucy pulling that football out at the last second for that sucker Charlie Brown and you've got the idea.

I guess what I'm saying is, be smoke, or at the very least be Lucy and pull that football away at the last moment so you can connect when your hapless Mr. Brown is flailing at air.

Blocking v parring

In pure technical terms, the most elite form of defense in striking is evasion. That is, not getting hit at all, as in no contact between you and your opponent whatsoever. Think of slipping, bobbing, weaving, ducking, elusive footwork, anything and everything that causes your opponent to bite nothing but air when he thought he was going to get a big ol' piece of you. Evasion is slick, beautiful stuff. Evasion is also one of the hardest skill sets for fighters to develop.

Elite evasion skills develop (if they ever do) after years of hardcore, deliberate drilling. The stopgap or stepping stone between getting hit and genuine evasive skills is contact defense. That is, defense where some form of contact between you and your opponent is demanded in order to ensure that you don't eat the full fury of the intended blow. Contact defense comes in two broad categories: blocking and parrying.

Blocking, as the name implies, involves placing a portion of your anatomy (preferably a less vulnerable portion) between your opponent's punch and his intended target. Blocking strikes to the head usually involves absorbing punches with the palms, forearms and/or upper arms. Strikes to the body are usually blocked with the forearms or upper arms.

Blocking has a lot to recommend it; most important being that it is the easiest of defensive skills to learn. If you have a modicum of discipline — holding a decent defensive shell is not that difficult — your blocking will come out of that shell. Blocking as a defense comes naturally to our species. Just think of winging a punch at an untrained fighter (don't do this, it's just a thought experiment) and picture how his arms will fly up to cover and protect his head. Bingo, that fighter is blocking and never even had a lesson.

There are some drawbacks to blocking. These drawbacks do not mean that you should not use blocking as a defensive tactic. I merely offer the drawbacks for your consideration.

Drawback numero uno: Every time you block you are essentially a one-armed fighter. A limb used in a defensive capacity for that fraction of a second cannot be used to launch offense. Sure, you can fire that limb right after you have used it to defend. I'm just saying if we add up all the fractions of seconds spent on a defensive strategy centered around blocking, we come up with a significant portion of your time being a one-armed fighter.

Better

Drawback numero dos: Blocking is still getting hit. Taking punches off of the arms is waaaaaaaaay better than blocking with your jaw, your nose, your ribs or your liver, but offensive contact to the body is still offensive contact. Blocking in early rounds can feel okey-doke, but ask those arms how they feel in later rounds. Check their responsiveness. Are they still as fast as they were before they accrued more than a few direct hits?

If blocking is the primitive, albeit effective, primary defensive skill and evasion the ne plus ultra, that puts parrying smack dab in the middle of this little hierarchy. Parrying is essentially a redirect of your opponent's punches. The parry takes incoming fire and diverts it away from the designated target or, at the very least, dissipates the power. Parrying is still a contact defense because to parry one must get one's hand(s) on a portion of the incoming limb to do the job. Parrying is superior to blocking in that, although there is contact, this

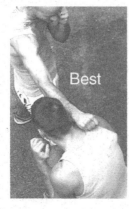

Best

contact is mitigated by how the parry interacts with the offensive limb.

Parrying has a drawback. It relies on being slightly out of position. That is, being cheated a little out of good defensive guard, and that means being a little vulnerable to attack. Think of it this way: Here comes that speedy jab at your face — if your rear hand is in good guard position, a little tuck and you have successfully blocked. To parry that same jab (to the inside or outside) you have to open that incoming jab line and then get your hand on either side of that punch to apply the redirect. Too slow? Uh-oh.

With the aforementioned pluses and minuses of blocking and parrying in mind, I suggest the following approach to building superior defensive skill.

1. Drill good guard position and do not deviate. Sure, its fun to watch elite fighters play the game with their hands low and tempting fate, but let's make sure you've mastered the rules before you break them.

2. From good guard position overlay your blocking skill set.

3. Drill parries for when you are cheated out of position. That is, for those times when you must defend when your own hand is en route for a punch or returning from a punch and are not in guard position. Save opening up lines to force a parry (drawing and the like) for later — trust me, we'll cover it.

4. From day one, all the while you are drilling guard position, your blocking and parrying, you will always have an eye on how to become evasive in upper body movement and footwork. Try to be evasive before you actually are. Try slipping that cross, but let's not get overconfident — put a block up ready to cover just in case you're not as good as you need to be. Work your bob and weave, but don't go all Pernell Whitaker with your hands down while you do it — you ain't Pernell Whitaker. Let's be safe while we try to emulate our betters.

So, there you go, four pragmatic steps to get you from flailing and flinching when someone swings at you to becoming evasive as smoke.

80/20 Rule (yet again)

As already stated, evasion is slicker than physical contact defenses (blocking, parrying, etc.), but we can't be 100 percent slick and hard to hit as smoke all the time. So, if we're going to make physical contact defense part of our game (which is unavoidable), is there anything to keep in mind before we get to defending? Yep.

In two previous books (*NHBF: The Book of Essential Submissions and NHBF: Savage Strikes*) we belabored the Pareto Principle, the 80/20 Rule, so we'll go light on the explanation here. Needless to say, (although I'm saying it all the same) if you aren't familiar with the Pareto Principle and how it applies to the fight game and find your appetite whetted by what is said here, have at look at the two aforementioned volumes.

The 80/20 Rule as it applies to boxing states that 80 percent of your defense will be conducted with the rear hand and 20 percent of your defense will be conducted with the lead hand.

The converse of the 80/20 Rule for Boxing states that 80 percent of your offense will be conducted with your lead hand and 20 percent of your offense with the rear hand.

Here's the wisdom behind the percentages. Putting most of the onus of physical contact defense on the rear hand (80 percent) leaves the lead hand free and clear to counter at will from its prime, up front, close and personal proximity to your opponent. Any time you use the lead hand to defend (unavoidable, but let's try and limit it to 20 percent) your rear hand counter has to travel further making it easier to read and be countered itself, and has to cross two limbs (your opponent's offensive hand and your defending lead hand) to make a bite on your target.

The wisdom of the 80/20 Rule is pretty tight, and yet there is an inevitable (and understand-able) tendency by novice boxers to want to use the lead hand to defend. This lead hand defense thing is a reflexive action. I mean, your brain sees some violence coming its way and throws up the nearest thing in its path (the lead hand) to save yourself. Again, nice reflexive action for everyday life, but in the sport of boxing, a reflex that must be rewired to the far more useful 80/20 ratio.

How-to x 2
Great news! I'm almost done yakking.

Part one: Defenses for all punches and angles
This book is broken into two parts. The first part is an encyclopedic checklist of all possible defenses for each punch and each specific angle of attack. These defenses have not been chosen willy-nilly. They are specific choices made by great defensive masters of the past and present.

You do not have to master all the defensive choices for each given punch, but I urge you to drill them all with equal attention, at least in the initial stages of your counterboxing journey. As you move further up the skill mastery road, you will experience a natural culling as you settle on the particular choices that make up your individual style.

Part two: Pragmatic first measures
The second half of the book deals with Pragmatic first measures that are the quickest, smartest and most logical counterpunch(es) that dovetail directly out of a specific defense and particular angle. Again, these are not slapdash choices. These are specific tried and true

choices made by our boxing betters.

The goal is to unite the two sections and to think of each specific defense as a trigger. You should drill so diligently that each specific defense elicits an immediate counterpunching response. To get to this rarefied ability, I suggest using a drill template illustrated in the following example.

Defensive choice:
Versus a **high jab,** work the **jab catch** for a minimum of three rounds.

Pragmatic first measure:
Add the **return jab** triggered by your **jab catch** versus a **high jab** for a minimum of three rounds.

Add the smart counter combination ...

Using the above template on all defenses and Pragmatic first measures should set you on the path to good counterpunching ability. But we all know combinations are where it's at, so we can continue the above template by adding smart combination work to your Pragmatic first measure.

To do this we've provided Combination menus after the Pragmatic first measures section. Once you've worked your defense for 3 rounds and then your Pragmatic first measure for 3 rounds, go to the Combination menu section and select a combination that begins with your Pragmatic first measure and ladder the combination from there.

The following example builds on our **jab catch v high jab + return jab**.

1. I've worked 3 rounds of **jab catching** and 3 rounds of **jab catch + return jab**.

2. I've selected **jab / cross / lead hook** from the Combination menu.

3. I work 3 rounds of **jab catch / return jab / cross**.

4. Then I work 3 rounds of **jab catch / return jab / cross / lead hook**.

By the time I've finished this sequence, I've worked my logical defense for 12 rounds, my Pragmatic first measure for 9 rounds, and counter combination work for 6 rounds (3 with the cross, 3 more with the cross + lead hook).

Proceeding through the book in this manner will stave off staleness and build instinctual response.

Note
The cross, of course, is also known as a rear straight. Both terms are used in this book and refer to the same punch.

They said it

The man who has no imagination has no wings.
— Muhammad Ali

He can run, but he can't hide.
— Joe Louis

*The fight is won or lost far away from witnesses —
behind the lines, in the gym, and out there on the
road, long before I dance under those lights.*
— Muhammad Ali

A champion is someone who gets up when he can't.
— Jack Dempsey

*Boxing is the ultimate challenge. There's nothing that
can compare to testing yourself the way you do
every time you step in the ring.*
— Sugar Ray Leonard

The bigger they are, the harder they fall.
— Bob Fitzsimmons

*It is not the size of a man but the size of his heart
that matters.*
— Evander Holyfield

*Life doesn't run away from nobody. Life runs at
people.*
— Joe Frazier

1.
Defenses
per punch

Defenses for each punch and each angle are listed in order of ease of execution. That is, defenses toward the beginning of each section are for novice through pro levels. Those defenses found toward the end of each section move you closer to becoming smoke.

High jab defenses

Cage / pinch
● Simply keep your chin tucked and pinch your guard together. Receive the punch on paralleled forearms.

Covering
● This one has the appearance of unpreparedness, but it does the job in a pinch as long as you reset your guard quickly.
● Raise your rear arm to the horizontal position — forearm facing out.
● Drop the lead arm to horizontally cover your liver.
● Place the forehead in the crook of the rear arm to receive impact.

Catch
● Receive the punch in the palm of the rear hand.
● Give a light smack into and up to begin educating opening lines.
● Don't reach for punches, allow them to come to you. Reaching opens up more lines for attack.

Leverage block
● Think of this as a "missed" catch and you're on the right track.
● Use the forearm of the rear arm to drive up and out on your opponent's incoming jab.

Inside parry
● A parry is a slight redirect. Keep in mind it doesn't take much to redirect so don't over-compensate with your parries. A miss of an inch is as good as a mile.
● Use the inside edge of the palm/forearm to brush/pat the jab from the inside to the outside.
● Step inside and away from the attack. Angle your upper body away from the punch while you parry.

Outside parry
● Use the rear hand to cuff/tap the glove of the jab from the outside to the inside.
● Again, not much force is required to do the job.

High jab defenses

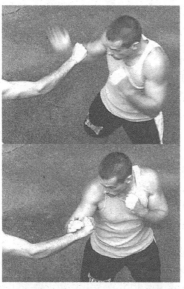

Cross parry
● A little 80/20 violation — use the lead hand to parry the jab from the inside to the outside.

Rear stopping/muffling
● Use the rear hand to "anticipate" a punch being fired.
● You will cover your opponent's lead glove with the palm of your own before it is fired.

Muffling/stopping is a key skill when using any upper body mobility (slips, ducks and weaves) to the inside position. Moving inside takes you into your opponent's power hand and a muffle on the rear hand is a nice safety.

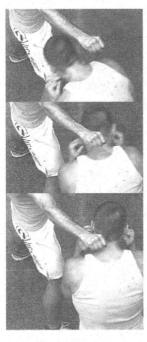

Slip inside
● To all appearances a slip looks like head movement to evade a punch. True, except that ...
● The head is moved in tandem with the body.
● To slip inside the high jab, turn your rear shoulder toward your lead knee, bend the knees and pivot toward the lead knee on the balls of both feet.

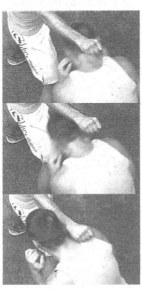

Slip outside
● Reverse the preceding instructions.
● Turn the lead shoulder toward the rear knee, bend the knees and pivot on the balls of your feet.

High jab defenses

Rear cuff down
● Think of cuffing as being a parry that travels along the vertical axis — up or down.
● Use the rear palm to cuff/brush the jab down.

Lead cuff down
● Use the lead hand this time.

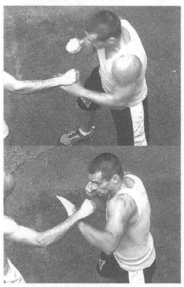

Rear cuff up
● Getting into a cuff up can feel a little artificial, but we drill it as a mighty useful defense when your hands are cheated into less than ideal position when your opponent's offense is launched.
● Use the back of the rear glove to brush/tap the punch upward.

Lead cuff up
● Use the lead hand this time.

We get into a few footwork options here — prime smoke material. For greater detail on developing your footwork, see our book *Boxer's Book of Conditioning & Drilling*.

Step back
● What it sounds like.
● Step the rear foot to the rear followed by the lead to reset your stance.

High jab defenses

Stance shift
● Simply step the lead foot rearward, in essence making your rear hand your new lead.

Quick shift

● Assuming you are properly stanced, drop the rear heel.

● Pivot on the ball of the rear foot toward your rear foot.

● At the same time drag the ball of the lead foot approximately 10 inches toward your rear foot (the inside ball of the foot will be facing the rear foot).

● Drive off the lead foot and take a step with your rear foot to your inside.

● Pivot toward your opponent and reset your stance.

● Sounds like a lot of steps, but this is an important step to becoming smoke.

High jab defenses

Rear shift

● Aside from the change in guard work, this is simply a quick shift to an alternate direction.

● Pivot toward the rear foot.

● Keep your eye on your opponent and go Bruce Lee, that is ...

● Lean back and drop the lead glove to cover your liver, your lead hand covers the lead side of the jaw — palm facing out.

● Drag the toes of the lead foot 10 inches toward the rear foot.

● Drive off the lead foot toes and step the rear foot to the rear.

● Reset your stance.

Drop shift

● Perhaps the toughest to master of the footwork evasions, but once you've got it down, it sets you up nicely for inside work.

● Hit a 1/4 squat on both legs.

● Drag the lead foot back approximately 8-10 inches ...

● Step the rear foot to the lead position and stand up.

High jab defenses

A few upper body evasions that require a bit more finesse than slipping.

Pull/roll

● Ideally, to roll or pull you keep your stance stock still to stay in punching range.

● Assuming a proper stance, drop your rear heel and lean toward your rear foot.

● Tighten your guard and take it with you.

● The rearward motion dissipates the force of the punch.

Snap back

● A snap back is simply a slicker roll or pull.

● Here your pull/roll implies that you have had to receive zero impact.

● Essentially they are the same motion, but we are splitting hairs to help you decide which is ideal for your own reach requirements.

Duck

● Hit a slight dip with the knees accompanied by a bend at the waist allowing the punch to pass overhead.

Folding

● A seldom seen today evasion from the old school — think of it as a duck with a safety added.
● Hit a 1/4 bend at the knees while bending forward at the waist.
● Throw both arms up with elbows angled toward the outside to knock the incoming punch up and/or to the outside.

High jab defenses

Weaving aka bob & weave

This is a highly useful skill used by some of the best.

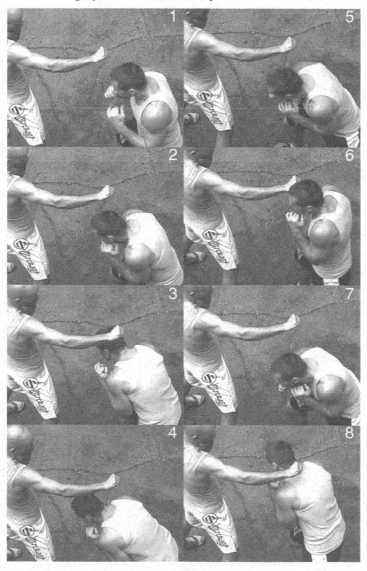

Weave form

It's worth breaking it into pieces
to get it right from the get-go.

● Think of the weave as
"weaving" together both forms of
the slip (inside to outside or vice
versa).
● Point the lead shoulder toward
the rear knee accompanied by a
slight waist bend.
● Keeping your waist bent, point
your rear shoulder toward your
lead knee and rise back to full
guard.
● Now reverse the motion. Point
the rear shoulder toward the lead
knee first, stay low and point the
lead shoulder toward the rear
knee and then rise.

High jab defenses

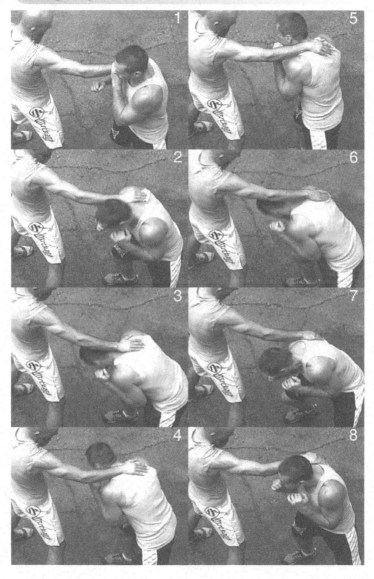

Weave partner drill #1

● Have your partner/coach stand in front of you and extend his arm placing the palm of his lead hand on top of your lead shoulder.

● Hit the preceding weave drill back and forth — his hand will travel from shoulder to shoulder across the back of your neck as you drill.

High jab defenses

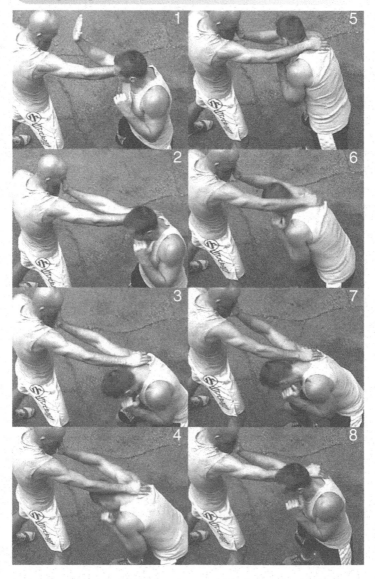

Weave partner drill #2

● Weaving can put you in jeopardy of eating your opponent's opposite hand, so it is wise to muffle/stop your partner's rear hand.

● Here, you will drill as in Weave Partner Drill #1, but your partner will hold his rear hand in guard.

● At the start of each weave cycle, place your open lead glove on top of his rear hand.

High jab defenses

1 Now using the weave against the High Jab.

Weave to the inside

● Weave from outside of the punch to the inside position.

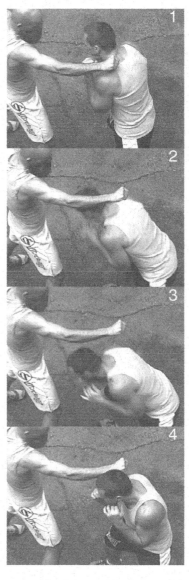

Weave to the outside

● You know what to do.

Low jab defenses

I provided you with lots of options for defending the high jab because it is far and away the most utilized punch in boxing (and for good reason). You need good answers for an offense that you will see every single time you step into the ring.

You will encounter the low jab less often, but is wise to stop here and ponder why we will encounter it. The jab to the body is not a finisher. It is a relatively weak punch and usually not intended to do major damage. The low jab is primarily used to bring the defender's hands down to set up the head. Let's keep that in mind as we drill the following defensive options.

Rear elbow block
● Your go-to defense for the low jab.
● Assuming you are still in good guard position, turn your body toward the inside as a unit to receive the blow off the rear elbow.
● Essential: Move the body, not the elbow — maintain good guard at all times.

Lead elbow block
● Performed as above moving the body to receive the blow on the lead elbow, but I urge you to use the rear elbow block more (approximately 80 percent) so the lead arm is ready to counter ASAP.

Low fold or Forearm block
● Risky as it leaves the chin open, but it is (and has been) used successfully by many counterboxing wizards.
● Stack the forearms in front of the body target areas — the rear forearm on top of the lead.
● Receive the blow on the forearms and get back to high guard immediately.

Rear low parry / rear low brush
● Essentially a sweep against the punch from the inside to the outside line.
● The upper arm stays pretty much in the same place since the rear forearm does the work. Think of your elbow as being the pivot point of a ball-and-socket joint and you're good to go.

Lead low parry / lead low brush
● The same mechanics as above with the lead arm.

Low jab defenses

Post and step away

● An old school defense used quite successfully by quick boxers and/or those with an appreciable range advantage.

● Post the open lead glove on the head of your opponent.

● At the same time, shuffle-slide your lead foot back a few inches.

● Swing the rear leg back to accent and assist your lead foot shuffle.

● At the same time, apply a rear low parry/brush with the rear hand for safety.

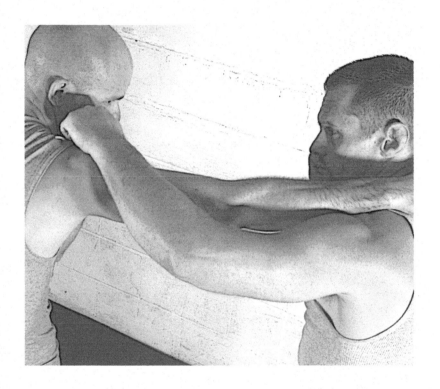

High rear straight defenses

Catch
● Use the open lead glove to receive the blow.
● Driving the caught blow a fraction upward and to your inside will open up countering angles.

Leverage block
● Use the lead arm to reach for your opponent's rear shoulder (inside his punching arm).
● Straightening your arm and turning your palm to the outside will keep your elbow high for better defense. Seems a bit awkward at first, but palm out will save your butt.

Lead inside parry

Lead outside parry

Cross parry

Shoulder roll
● All of the following happens simultaneously.
● Turn toward your inside.
● Raise your lead shoulder and place the lead glove over your liver.
● Raise the open rear glove to cover your chin.
● Lean slightly over the rear foot.
● Receive the blow on your lead delts.

High rear straight defenses

Slip inside

Slip outside

Step back

Circle away

● A preemptive footwork strategy.

● Keep your footwork tending to the inside to make your opponent constantly work to set the rear hand.

A note on circling away from the power hand (lead hooks and rear straights)

Often you can be preemptive about defense by circling. Circling in the case of defending against a lead hook is to keep your footwork circling and tending to the left versus an orthodox stance and circling/tending to the right versus a southpaw.

Circling is less about being reactive to a punch and more about planning ahead. There is a caveat regarding circling — circling away from a lead hook steps you into your opponent's rear straight while circling away from a rear straight steps you into your opponent's lead hook. This is a tough dilemma, but it does not mean you toss circling as a useful tool.

Choosing not to circle leaves your opponent set for both power shots — the lead hook and the rear straight. Your job is to do your homework. Know either from studying your opponent prior to the fight or with careful observation in early rounds to determine which of the two power shots is the baddest. Once you know which one to be most concerned with, circle appropriately.

High rear straight defenses

Crowding or circling into the rear hand

● Power and speed need room to generate. With that in mind, you can adopt a strategy of tending your footwork into your opponent's power hand and keeping it crowded so that it never has the room he needs to work to optimum.

● Keep your hands high if you adopt this tactic.

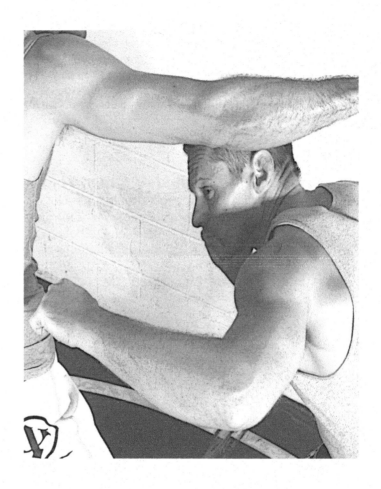

Low rear straight defenses

Essentially your low jab defensive arsenal.

Elbow block

● Simply block the blow with the lead elbow or forearm.
● As a rule, turn your body so that the elbow is in front of the blow as opposed to moving only your elbow.

Low fold or forearm block

● Place the forearms parallel and horizontal in front of the liver — lead forearm on the bottom.
● A risky one since it opens up the chin, but it has its place in the arsenal.

Lead brush

 *Rear brush*

 *Post and step away*

High lead hook defenses

Cover

● A bread and butter basic.

● Place the rear hand over your ear as if holding a phone while keeping your rear elbow vertical — winging the elbow out opens the body.

● Remember to take your head to your hand and not your hand to your head — lifting the elbow opens the body to attack, taking your head to your hand compacts your defense.

Duck

● Maintain good guard and hit a quick straight down drop underneath the attack.

● A duck moves as close to straight up and down as can be managed. Leaning forward while ducking opens up nasty uppercut opportunities for your opponent.

Step back

● Keep in mind a step back, unless accompanied by a quick step back in, usually nullifies or mitigates your countering opportunities.

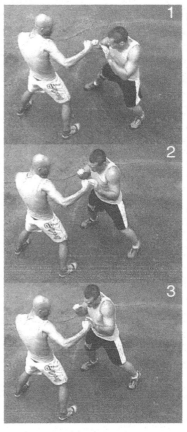

Circling
● Step the lead foot to the outside.
● Pivot on the lead foot resetting your stance away from your opponent's lead hook.

Low lead hook defense

Low fold
● Perform as you do with the lead fold versus the low jab.

High rear hook defenses

Shoulder stop
● Step into your opponent and place the lead hand on your opponent's rear shoulder.

Bicep stop
● Performed as above, but here the hand is placed on his rear biceps.

Duck

Block
● Think of the block as a long cover.
● Place the forearm between the rear hook and its target.

High rear hook defenses

1 *Circle away*

2

Step back

Low rear hook defense

Low fold

● When you fold against the rear low hook, turn the body as a unit to receive the punch as you fold.

Lead uppercut defenses

Uppercuts travel a vertical arc, and the actual target can be tough to determine. That is, is it fired to the body or head? These defenses will work in both target instances.

Step back or lean
● Merely stepping back or leaning away from an uppercut is often enough to do the job.

Brush
● Drop the rear hand down and to the outside sweeping his uppercut away.

Cross brush
● A little riskier because it exposes the chin.
● Drop the lead glove down on the uppercut and sweep it to the inside.

Chop

● Think of a chop as a brush with "oomph!" to it.

● With your rear forearm, chop down HARD on the wrist of the uppercut arm.

Rear uppercut defenses

Duplicate the low lead uppercut defense and you're good to go.

Lead brush

Lead chop
or forearm block

Step back

2. Pragmatic first measures

Not every single possible counter per punch is shown here, but rather an exhaustive reference of the highest scoring returns used by the best counter boxers the sport has produced.

High jab first measures

Return jab
● A return jab is exactly what it sounds like — your opponent jabs and you return your own jab.
● The best counter boxer treats his opponent's offense as a trigger for his own. Keep this immediate response in mind throughout.

Cage / pinch to return jab

Cover to return jab

Catch to return jab

High jab first measures

Riding the jab
● This is essentially rolling or snapping back with the jab and firing the return jab on your return to position.

Inside parry to return jab

Inside parry to return jab with inside step

● Use footwork to get closer to your opponent. This will add more stink to your punches and shorten his offense, thus mitigating his power.

● Hit your inside parry while taking a short step forward and inside.

Outside parry pin to return jab

● The pin is not essential, but it is a nice bonus if you can make it stick.

● Use your outside parry to slap pin his extended jab against the deltoid of your return jab arm.

● No worries if the slap-pin doesn't occur. We just need the punch to miss and our return jab to bite. The pin is gravy if it happens.

High jab first measures

Outside parry pin to return jab plus forward step

● Sometimes a forward step timed with your outside parry sticks the pin a bit better.

Outside parry pin to return jab plus drop shift

● This is an ideal opportunity for the seldom used drop shift.
● Time the drop shift with your outside parry — this puts you completely on the outside of your opponent.

Outside parry to lead uppercut
● Hit your outside parry.
● Step the rear foot forward and to the outside.
● Bang the body with the lead uppercut.

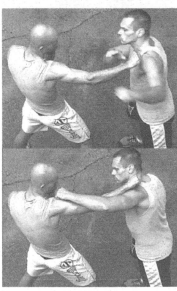

Cross the jab
● A beautiful counter that takes a bit of practice, but well worth the time.
● Step slightly forward and inside with the lead foot while slipping to the inside of his jab.
● Throw the rear hand over the top of his jab aiming for his jaw.
● In ideal execution, his extended jab will be over your rear shoulder while your rear hand crosses over the top of the jab from the outside.
● A stop on his rear hand with your lead is recommended.

High jab first measures

Inside straight

● Think of this as a cross on the inside line.

● Take a short step as in the cross.

● Throw the rear straight to the chin, but cheat the rear shoulder a bit more toward your centerline than you might normally to create an inside slip.

Inside straight to body

● Same as in the preceding, but here the target is the liver or heart.

● Don't punch downhill. Change levels with your straight so that you are punching straight out from your shoulder.

Inside parry to rear straight

● Step slightly forward and to the outside.
● Parry the jab outward with the rear hand.
● Drive the rear straight directly from where the parry ends.

Leverage block to rear hook

● Hit your leverage block and then drive the rear hook from exactly where your block ends — no need to draw back.
● A short step forward and to the inside with the lead will add some stink to your hook.

High jab first measures

Rear outside guard to rear hook to chin

● A longer version of the pre-ceding.

● Slip a bit inside and use the forearm to block the punch.

● Raise the rear elbow and fire the hook from here.

Outside parry with shuffle in lead hook

● Outside parry while taking a short shuffle-step forward and inside.

● Fire the lead hook to the chin.

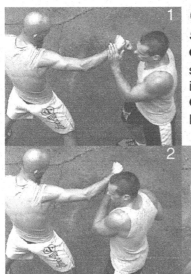

Outside parry with shuffle in lead uppercut
● Outside parry while taking a short shuffle-step forward and inside.
● Fire the lead uppercut to the liver.

Outside parry with stance shift to lead uppercut
● Outside parry with the rear hand while ...
● Stance shifting forward and outside of his jab.
● Fire an uppercut to the body with the former lead hand (non-parry hand).

High jab first measures

Rear cuff up to lead uppercut

● As you hit the cuff up, take a slight shuffle step forward and inside with the lead foot.
● At the same time, lean over that lead leg to load your uppercut.
● Fire to the liver.

Cross parry to rear straight to the chin

● Cross parry knocking your opponent's jab to the outside line.
● Fire your rear hand to his jaw.

Cross parry to rear straight to body

● Set up as before, but here hit a 1/4 squat and bang the heart or liver.

Cross parry to rear hook to chin

High jab first measures

Cross parry to rear uppercut to body

Outside slip to low jab

The low jab is a bit slight in power and not a prime counter in this situation, but there are a couple of options that have been used successfully by some. Here's one.

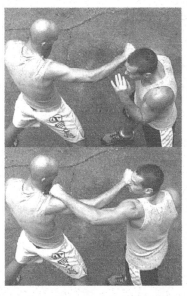

Outside slip to rear straight to chin

● Here you'll have the advantage of having the rear straight cocked off the slip.

Outside slip to rear hook to chin

High jab first measures

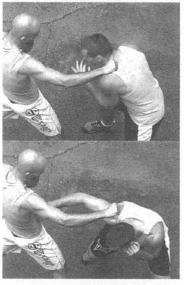

Inside slip to low jab
● You'll have to shuffle step slightly forward and to the inside for this one.

Inside slip to rear corkscrew hook to chin

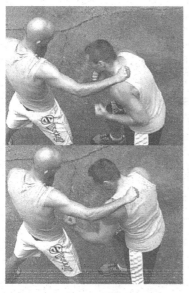

Inside slip to rear uppercut to body

Rear inside parry to lead uppercut

● Add a little slip to the inside as you hit your parry to better set up your uppercut.

High jab first measures

Here are two 3-point combinations for the high jab to the chin that are well worth getting down cold.

Inside triple

● Slip inside the high jab and fire a rear straight to the heart.

● Weave under the jab and hook the solar plexus with the lead hand.

● Pop up and cross the jab with a rear straight to the chin.

Outside triple
- A Jack Dempsey favorite.
- Slip outside the high jab and fire a lead hook to the liver.
- Rear hook to the liver or short ribs.
- Pop up to a lead uppercut to the chin.

Low jab first measures

Lead low parry to rear straight to body
● Sweep that jab wide and bang the now open body.

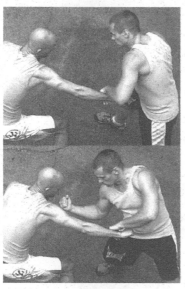

Rear low parry to lead uppercut

Lead low parry to rear uppercut

High rear straight first measures

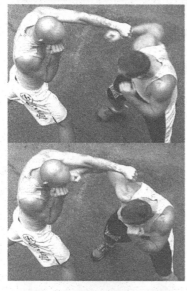

Slip inside with short lead hook to chin

● There won't be much travel to this hook, but your opponent meeting it does the job.

Slip outside rear straight to heart or liver

**Slip outside to rear
uppercut to body**

**Rear cross parry to lead
hook to chin**

High rear straight first measures

Rear cross parry to lead uppercut

Lead cross parry pin to return rear straight
● Accompanied by a short step with the lead foot forward and to the outside adds some power to this counter.

Lead cross parry pin to rear uppercut to liver

● Same mechanics as in the preceding, but different return fire.

Lead inside parry to rear straight to chin

High rear straight first measures

Lead inside parry to rear uppercut to liver

Lead outside parry to rear uppercut to liver

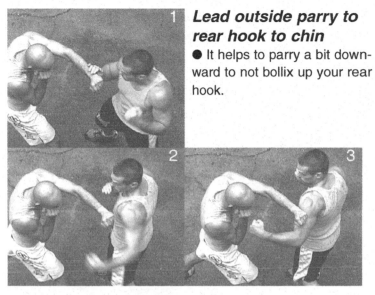

Lead outside parry to rear hook to chin

● It helps to parry a bit downward to not bollix up your rear hook.

Rear cross parry to lead uppercut to liver

High rear straight first measures

Rear cross parry to lead hook to chin

Rear step outside to jab to chin

Rear step inside to lead hook to chin

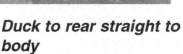

Duck to rear straight to body
● Take a short step to the inside while ducking to add to your power.

Low rear straight first measures

Jab as a stop hit

Step inside to lead uppercut
● Step the rear foot inside and bang the body or chin with the lead uppercut.

Step inside to lead hook to chin

Lead brush to rear uppercut

High lead hook first measures

Jab stop hit to chin

● A stop hit is essentially beating your opponent to the punch. Your straight jab will travel faster than the arcing hook (assuming you've timed it well).

Rear straight stop hit to chin

● Here you will find that a short step forward and to the inside with your lead foot will assist the blow's power.

Rear straight stop hit to body

● Use the same footwork as in the stop hit to the chin.

Cover return hook
● Defend with a cover, step forward and inside with the lead foot.
● Wheel the rear foot to reposition inside and fire your own lead hook.
● Think of this as all one motion.

Cover lead uppercut to body
● Use the same footwork as the return hook.

High lead hook first measures

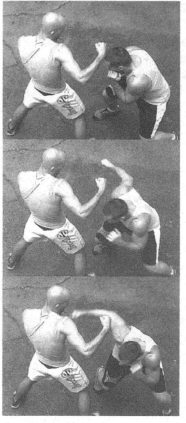

Duck to lead hook to body

● As you duck, step forward and outside with the rear foot to really dig that body hard.

High rear hook first measures

Jab stop hit
● Step in and fire the speedier jab to the chin.

Step inside to lead uppercut
● As you read the rear hook, step the rear foot forward.
● Fire your lead uppercut to the liver.

High rear hook first measures

Rear straight to body

● As you read the rear hook, step forward and fire the rear straight.
● As long as you aren't punching downhill, the rear hook will pass overhead.

Jab to body

● Step into your opponent and fire the jab to the liver.

Lead block to return rear hook

● As you read the rear hook, step inside and block with the lead forearm.
● Fire back with your own rear hook.

Lead uppercut first measures

All brushes can be chops.

Rear brush to jab to chin
● Step forward with the jab to add stink.

Rear brush to return lead uppercut

Lead uppercut first measures

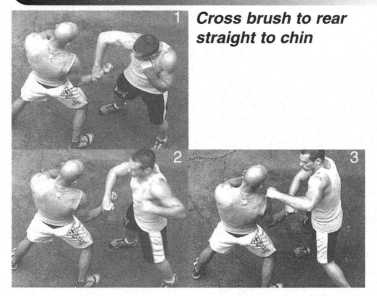

Cross brush to rear straight to chin

Cross brush to rear hook to chin

Rear uppercut first measures

Jab to chin as a stop hit

Lead hook to chin as a stop hit

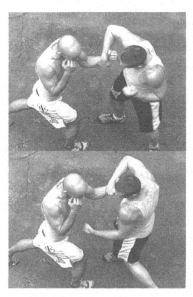

Lead brush to return rear uppercut

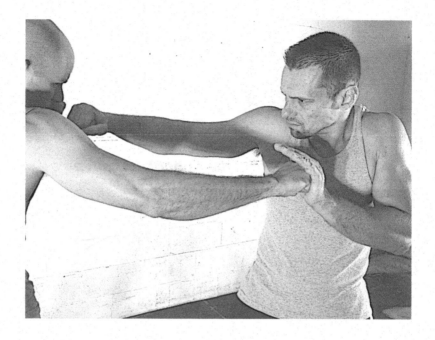

3.
Combination menus

Like I said earlier, use the Combination menus after the Pragmatic first measures section. Once you've worked your defense for three rounds and your Pragmatic first measure for three rounds, go to the Combination menu section and select a combination that begins with your Pragmatic first measure and ladder the combination from there.

We've broken the menus down according to which punch opens the combination to assist your referencing.

If you need a refresher on the prescribed method, see pages 48-51.

If a punch target is not designated (e.g., chin or head), it is fired to the head.

Jab to chin start combos

Double jab to chin

Jab head / Jab body

Jab chin / Cross chin

Jab chin / Cross body

Jab chin / Lead hook chin

Jab chin / Rear uppercut

Jab chin / Lead uppercut

Triple jab

Jab to chin start combos

Jab / Lead hook / Rear uppercut

Jab / Rear uppercut / Lead hook

Jab / Jab / Cross

Jab head / Jab body / Lead hook head

Jab / Cross / Lead hook

Jab / Cross / Rear uppercut

Jab / Lead hook / Rear hook

Jab head / Cross body / Lead hook head

Jab to chin start *combos*

Jab / Cross / Jab

Jab / Lead uppercut / Lead hook

Jab / Lead hook / Cross

Jab / Lead hook / Lead uppercut

Jab / Lead hook body / Lead hook head

Jab / Rear uppercut / Rear hook head

Jab / Cross /
Lead hook body / Rear uppercut

Jab to chin start combos

Jab / Lead hook /
Cross / Lead hook

Jab / Lead hook body /
Lead hook head / Rear uppercut

Jab / Cross body /
Lead hook / Rear hook body

Double jab high /
Jab low / Lead hook (high)

Jab to body start combos

Jab body / Jab head

Double jab body

Jab body / Cross chin

Jab body / Cross body

Jab body / Lead hook chin

Jab body / Rear hook chin

Cross to chin start *combos*

Cross chin / Lead hook chin

Cross chin / Lead hook body

Cross / Lead hook / Cross

Cross / Lead hook /
Cross / Lead hook body

Cross / Lead hook /
Cross body / Lead uppercut

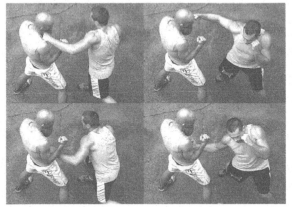

Cross to body start combos

Cross body / Lead hook chin

Cross body / Lead hook body / Cross chin

Lead hook to chin start combos

Lead hook chin / Rear uppercut

Lead hook chin / Cross body

Lead hook chin / Rear hook chin

Lead hook chin / Lead uppercut

Lead hook to chin start *combos*

Lead hook / Cross / Lead hook

Lead hook / Rear uppercut / Cross

Lead hook / Rear uppercut / Rear hook

Lead hook / Rear hook / Rear uppercut / Lead uppercut

Lead hook / Rear uppercut / Rear hook / Lead uppercut

Lead hook to chin start *combos*

Lead hook / Lead uppercut / Rear uppercut / Rear hook

Lead hook to body start *combos*

Double lead hooks (first to head, second to body)

Lead hook body / Lead hook head / Lead uppercut

Lead hook body / Rear hook body / Lead uppercut

Rear hook to chin start combo

Rear hook chin / Lead uppercut

Rear hook to body start combo

Double rear hook (first to body, second to head)

Lead uppercut start *combos*

Lead uppercut / Jab chin

Lead uppercut / Rear hook chin

Lead uppercut / Rear uppercut

Lead uppercut / Rear hook / Lead hook

Lead uppercut start *combos*

Lead uppercut / Lead hook / Rear uppercut / Rear hook

Rear uppercut start combos

Rear uppercut / Lead hook chin

Rear uppercut / Cross chin

Rear uppercut / Jab chin

Rear uppercut / Rear hook chin

Conclusion

OK, that's enough for this one. To reiterate, if you use our first book in this series, *Boxing Mastery*, to school the fundamentals, couple that with *Boxer's Book of Conditioning & Drilling* and then add this volume on counter fighting. You have more than enough tools to move you from novice to one slippery and canny sweet scientist. To be honest, the only things I can think to add to ensure pugilistic excellence would be an exposition on "forcing" (drilling for feints, drawing, shifting, et cetera); Ring Generalship (overall strategy as opposed to tactics); and specific game plans for facing disparate classes of fighters (southpaws, tall fighters, rushers, runners, in-fighters, et cetera). But we'll leave that for another day.

In the meantime, you have more than enough with these three volumes to get you to where you want and need to go. If you have any question regarding the material, feel free to contact me via the address below. You can also visit our website and sign up for our free weekly newsletter, which offers more drilling ideas and videos to keep your progress on the fast track.

Thanks and keep punching!
Mark Hatmaker
mark@extremeselfprotection.com
www.extremeselfprotection.com

Resources

BEST CHOICES
First, please visit my website at
www.extremeselfprotection.com
You will find even more training
material as well as updates and
other resources.

Amazon.com
The place to browse for books such
as this one and other similar titles.

Paladin Press
www.paladin-press.com
Paladin carries many training
resources as well as some of my
videos, which allow you to see
much of what is covered in my
NHB books.

Ringside Boxing
www.ringside.com
Best choice for primo equipment.

Sherdog.com
Best resource for MMA news, event
results and NHB happenings.

Threat Response Solutions
www.trsdirect.com
They also offer many training
resources along with some of my
products.

Tracks Publishing
www.trackspublishing.com
They publish all the books in the
NHBF series and MMA series as
well as a few fine boxing titles.

www.humankinetics.com
Training and conditioning info.

www.matsmatsmats.com
Best resource for quality mats at
good prices.

Video instruction

Extreme Self-Protection
extremeselfprotection.com

Paladin Press
paladin-press.com

Threat Response Solutions
trsdirect.com

World Martial Arts
groundfighter.com

Events

IFC
ifc-usa.com

IVC
valetudo.com

King of the Cage
kingofthecage.com

Pancrase
so-net.ne.jp/pancrase

Pride
pridefc.com

The Ultimate Fighting
Championships
ufc.tv

Universal Combat Challenge
ucczone.ca/

Index

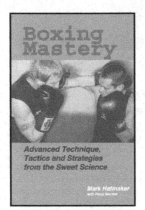

Boxing Mastery
Advance Techniques, Tactics and Strategies from the Sweet Science
Advanced boxing skills and ring generalship.
978-1-884654-29-9 / $12.95
900 photos

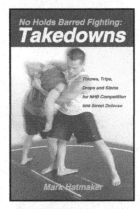

No Holds Barred Fighting: Takedowns
Throws, Trips, Drops and Slams for NHB Competition and Street Defense
978-1-884654-25-1 / $12.95
850 photos

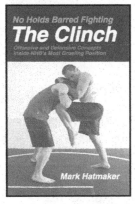

No Holds Barred Fighting: The Clinch
Offensive and Defensive Concepts Inside NHB's Most Grueling Position
978-1-884654-27-5 / $12.95
750 photos

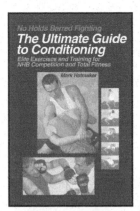

No Holds Barred Fighting:
The Ultimate Guide to Conditioning
Elite Exercises and Training for NHB
Competition and Total Fitness
978-1-884654-29-9 / $12.95
900 photos

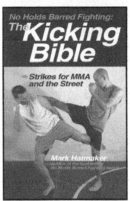

No Holds Barred Fighting:
The Kicking Bible
Strikes for MMA and the Street
978-1-884654-31-2 / $12.95
700 photos

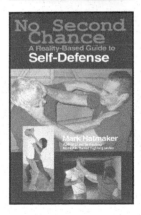

No Second Chance:
A Reality-Based Guide to Self-Defense
How to avoid and survive an assault.
978-1-884654-32-9 / $12.95
500 photos

**No Holds Barred Fighting:
The Book of Essential Submissions**
How MMA champions gain their victories. A catalog of winning submissions.
978-1-884654-33-6 / $12.95
750 photos

**MMA Mastery: Flow Chain Drilling
and Integrated O/D Training
to Submission Wrestling**
Blends all aspects of the MMA fight game into devastating performances.
978-1-884654-38-1 / $13.95
800 photos

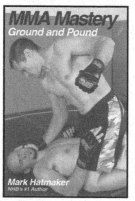

MMA Mastery: Ground and Pound
A comprehensive go-to guide — how to win on the ground.
978-1-884654-39-8 / $13.95
650 photos

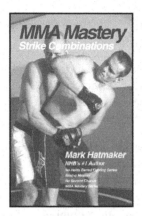

MMA Mastery: Strike Combinations
Learn the savage efficiency of striking in combinations. A comprehensive guide.
978-1-935937-22-7 / $12.95
1,000 photos

Boxer's Book of Conditioning & Drilling
How to get fighting fit like the champions.
978-1-935937-28-9 / $13.95
650 photos

Mark Hatmaker is the bestselling author of the *No Holds Barred Fighting Series,* the *MMA Mastery Series, No Second Chance* and *Boxing Mastery.* He also has produced more than 40 instructional

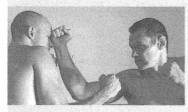

videos. His resume includes extensive experience in the combat arts including boxing, wrestling, Jiu-jitsu and Muay Thai.

He is a highly regarded coach of professional and amateur fighters, law enforcement officials and security personnel. Hatmaker founded Extreme Self Protection (ESP), a research body that compiles, analyzes and teaches the most effective Western combat methods known. ESP holds numerous seminars throughout the country each year including the prestigious Karate College/Martial Arts Universities in Radford, Virginia. He lives in Knoxville, Tennessee.

www.extremeselfprotection.com